WHAT WE'VE COME HERE FOR

ACKNOWLEDGMENTS

I would like to thank my husband, Rick; our family, friends and colleagues; the poets and writers of Arizona State University, notably Beckian Fritz Goldberg, Alberto Álvaro Ríos, Norman Dubie, Jewell Parker Rhodes and Jeannine Savard; Karla Elling; the late, great Jim Green; Gregory Castle; Michael Vanden Heuvel; Carolyn Forché; Helene Rollins; Meg and Jim Files; and Elena and Jim Thornton. Without their love and support, this chapbook would not be possible.

ISBN No. 978-0-9861200-9-1 "What We've Come Here For"

© "Summertime at the Trailer, Near Alpine, Arizona," June 2006, photograph by Richard Dyer

WHAT WE'VE COME HERE FOR

Poems by

Rebecca Dyer

For our parents

Bill and Derry
Dick and Joan

TABLE OF CONTENTS

SECTION ONE

These Waters..3

SECTION TWO

The Manatee..13

MemoryJungle..14

Twin...16

Possibilities in Trees...17

The Big Tree..18

Garden of Absolutes..19

SECTION THREE

Tucson Trilogy

Living on Miracle Mile..23

Trees Without Leaves...25

Light Housekeeping...26

SECTION FOUR

Himmel..31

WHAT WE'VE COME HERE FOR

SECTION ONE

These Waters

For Jodie

My grandmother's eyes
the blue-green algae of the stream.
She was the first to drink.

Only when we must
my father
and I

follow this road
far from what we know.
I cannot find

from the highway where it begins.
The road is not on any map.
My father remembers.

We turn a bend I would miss
and are upon it.
A gooseberry bush chokes shut the gate.

My father's fingers bleed
prying it open. This road full of grooves
has never been paved.

Our low-slung Plymouth
slides side to side, a fat
white horse shying.

It's all right, my father says,
pulling the Plymouth back.
It's all right as long as it doesn't rain.

We got stuck in that meadow,
in the mud, he says. Remember.
Your Uncle Hack and I

dug out the car. Took all day.
You kids hiked
back to the cabin with Mom.

We jumped over giant red anthills,
I say. I remember.
The field was covered with them.

Just like Mars. Giant red ants
crawled all over. They sting
the worst. My father nods:

We just bought you new boots.
Good thing, too, I say.
My father laughs and settles

into the sliding of the car.
Only we come down this road.
It will take us

from my mother,
my sisters and brothers.
We follow it for them.

Once my brother
drank these waters
he never left.

My father says a bear sipped
where the stream begins above ground.
My brother is like a bear:

Moss and pine
needles cling to his back.
He scoops and swallows

rainbow whole. Fish bones stick
in his throat, years of bone
impale his gullet. He hacks

and chokes until dark waters
soothe. I have forgotten
his scent.

This road furrowed
like my father's face
takes us to the stream.

Pines nude from the waist
down block any sun,
aspen leaves quiver,

unable to reconcile their light
and dark sides. The gooseberry's deep purple
thorn alone beside the green berry.

Blue jays of sunlit meadows,
they are not here. The red
flash of a woodpecker

does not stay. For what warmth
filters through, a timber rattler
stretches its belly

up and out on a flat white rock.
But the stream is what we've come here for,
what we can pull from it.

So cold, these waters.
Black silt like silk. Centuries have made
the brown stones. Rainbow

hide in their shadows.
These trout won't take any bait.
They must bite your fingers.

You must lure them, imitating
fat worms, tiny guts seeping blood.
These trout must bite your fingers.

An elk once stood
where my sister drank.
My sister, nervous

and stamping,
became an elk.
I was still for her.

She approached. I stretched.
I would have touched her.
She blended with the trees.

Her hoof print, her pebble-sized droppings
I tracked to higher ground.
She sought deeper streams.

My father has mastered the rainbow,
pulling it from dark waters,
lured and with line, sacrifices

fingers only when he must.
The brown storm that turns
the trees and rocks

does not frighten him.
Hooking trout is all.
He will split them, clean

them, strip them of bone
in a ritual I have seen since childhood.
My father has mastered the rainbow.

A dying fish lying in the kitchen
is a great weight on the drain board.
A knife slides down the middle,

green scales that could cut
fingers ripple away
expose pink flesh.

The head is yanked back.
With it the spine, large bones
and a sharp odor of life

spent feeding on algae.
The rainbow is washed, left to drain.
Blood and water drip

from its tail.
Tonight my mother
fries rainbow in cornmeal.

I pick my fish apart, fearing
bones I cannot see.
Jesus fed the masses

this bread, this fish.
A bone sticks in my throat.
I want to choke.

Eat bread,
my mother tells me,
wash it down.

Chew them well,
my father says, that's all.
These bones are small.

My grandmother has mastered the end,
going where morphine
takes her, giving out shallow

breaths, lips flapping over false teeth
unhooked from gums.
Earlier they split her,

took two-thirds of her
and still couldn't get
the cancer. Soon my mother

will give more of the clear,
forgiving liquid to my grandmother,
moving beyond dark waters.

One night in the beginning
we camped beside the stream.
I connected stars with my fingers.

My grandmother swam the night,
drank from its currents.
My grandmother became a fox.

Daybreak a fox with silver nose
smelled our tent flap. I looked
into my grandmother's eyes.

Without shoes I followed her,
kept my grandmother at a distance.
She sniffed beside the stream,

followed it even as it went underground, uphill,
snout skimming rocks and logs,
a magnet pulled along an iron spike.

I tracked my grandmother to a cave.
I do not think she saw me.
I watched her sip water

bubbling out of rocks,
slap back and forth
blind white fish in pools

then slowly eat one.
Today I cup my hand
under the water to drink.

My father pulls me away.
He tells me the fish are biting.
His hook and line

split the water, a red lure
pops to the surface.
My father leans back and waits.

The hook takes a mouth,
line that cannot be broken
drags the catch in.

SECTION TWO

The Manatee

An ars poetica
For Maurya Simon

It is not that there is a new imagination but that there is a new reality. — *Wallace Stevens*

Spooning currents like a new-found lover,
slow-breathing stone dropping into deeper canyons.
Memories push to the front: Ancestors thundering across savannas,
dry grasses thrashing their bellies.

You float to the surface in an afterthought,
sipping air like a Chinese scholar.
Glaucoma-misted, no mermaid,
you bump into a schooner rib, splintering your muzzle.

Hyacinth-entwined, you graze in peace,
leaving your scent for others, calling into the distance.
Your closest kin, the elephants, reply,
shedding their legs at your shore.

Memory Jungle

For Aunt Ruthie

I am the guest you last
remember as a pudgy
grandniece — you love
even as I nudge open

French doors to your
backyard jungle where
albino peacocks fan
the edges, a mynah shrieks

stories from the porch.
A rubber-nosed monkey mugs
faces you'd rather forget.
I've let the yard go —

stooped, you lean on me down
the steps — *but have
a look, it's all junk
anyway.* You raise your

head, imperceptibly palsied.
Eyes blue and bulging
say, *Don't bullshit me,
I haven't the time.* You cough

jaggedly. *Damned cigarettes, can't
stop now.* You looked 50 for 20
years, aged a lifetime in the past
four. *Your grandmother didn't*

*know me that last
day. Doesn't matter
now. I have her
ashes under the gazebo*

next to Mama's
poetry book, Papa's
lit cigar. I'm careful not
to mix the ashes.

You cackle and a gazelle
springs for cover.
She's in the blue
bottle, to catch the light.

From ivy shade, two
emeralds glitter. A shadow
purrs like a generator,
crosses over a sun-

dial. *Don't be scared, it's my*
protection. If you look
closely you can still
see its spots.

Twin

Before the knowledge of I
is the sense of other.

Other-than-I and I
breathe the same blood,

are torn from the same fruit.
We kick our soft walls.

Circle each other like boxers,
grapple and pull apart.

Distance vibrates our chamber,
the inhale and the exhale

sway us to sleep, one
heart shadowing another.

Possibilities in Trees

For Katie Lumia

The child sees possibilities in trees:
Only if you climb one does the bark
feel like your mother's rough sole,
the root looks like her hammertoe.
You shinny up, gladly giving your skin.
You hang from a limb
and the ground would pull you down,
but the tree won't let you go.

Light shining through leaves blinds you.
Wind blowing through trees is more honest.
The tree never gets sick, never gets tired.
In its shadows no one can see you.
The tree will always take you in its arms
and never stops singing.
You are no longer a part of anything
that is not tree.

The Big Tree
Burned in the Wallow Fire of 2011

Up the mountain, far back in the woods,
the world's biggest tree grows.
It does not tower over other pines,
it is not so tall as it is wide:
Fingers at the end of forty arms
circled around would barely touch.
The forest thins out near this ancient tree
patiently spinning rings. No path leads here.
If you must seek it out,
pack a bedroll, fire, food and water for seven days.
An old mining shack leans against the mountain,
behind it melting snows have carved a ravine. Follow it.
Logs and limbs, broken stones clutter the gash
like an enemy battlefield. Step carefully.
Pull yourself up with the young, strong ferns rooted in the ledges.
Snap any skeletal branches of uprooted trees in your way.
At some point you will reach flat ground.
Stay close to an old fence — it keeps cattle from straying.
You should find the clearing within three days.
Do not expect to take home mementos, none will be found.
Squirrels hide the pine's seeds,
you cannot saw the iron branches.
Initials carved in the trunk grow over in a day.
Do not bother trying to start a fire, the needles never dry.
When you finally go,
and you will go,
leave nothing of yourself.

Garden of Absolutes

For LTR

No light, no life
but what we bring
to a garden of absolute blackness.
Our voices are rivers
plowing newborn beds.
On this ground we scatter our first teeth.
When we tend, we breathe without air.

Mothers' voices murmur at midnight,
in the garden moonsongs flow comforting
children's shadows jagged and broken on iron fences.
Even in moonlight there are shadows.
Silver dust falls like rain,
caresses a chair ceasing to rock.
Left alone a telescope turns inward.
A spun-glass angel, feathers crushed.
Whatever grows in our garden grows painfully.

Outside these fences water seeks itself.
Moontides forever lapping lapping,
pooling onto this stony shore,
where glass cuts twin brown moons from rock.

Blood plum stolen from sunset
hanging heavy on the trees
rises naked and white. It reaches the center of our blackness.
When we breathe, light so frozen cracks our ribs.
Silver plum shattering into one-hundred mirrored slivers:
What was not begins flowing,
what could not begins.

SECTION THREE

Tucson Trilogy

For my grandmother

Living on Miracle Mile

You're week-to-week at the Deseret Inn,
down the strip from Motel Marilyn
where a blue-suited lady trailing neon
dives nightly into asphalt.
A cooler stuck in the window
freezes the toes of your broken leg.
An unreachable itch crawls up and down like ants.
Saturdays, your grandchildren swim in the kidney-shaped pool
as you drowse in the afternoons of a Tucson October.

That summer of orientation, Philadelphia '69,
you couldn't tell the boys from the girls, so much hair.
A chartered flight across the Atlantic, cocktails and T-bone steaks.
You were learning West African dialects when you slipped
down rain-drenched steps on the way to breakfast.
You flew home first-class, first off the plane in a wheelchair,
leg stuck out like a tipped flamingo,
Peace Corps dreams running in the puddles of Freetown.

Now the widower next door
totters into your life like a stray bull terrier.
He's a decade younger,
a 50-year-old hippie driving a blue and white VW van.
You feel like his mother,
but barbecues beside the pool, violent red sunsets
have you hopeful for the future.
At night as you doze in bed alone
pink saguaros from the motel sign
bleed through your curtains.
The room's corners flicker with black and white TV shadows.
You dream of Mark, haven't thought of him in days.

The extra pillow nuzzles your neck,
you reach for him, wake up whimpering.
In the morning, they cut your leg from its plaster cocoon,
the skin brown and wrinkled like the Sierra Leone deltas,
pungent with possibilities. You plan your next trip for Africa.

Trees Without Leaves

Winter parches our skulls,
clings to our throats like the dry cough
you've had since November.
One afternoon playing bridge
you take off your wig for good.
North of Picacho leafless pecans
pierce a dull sky.

Mornings you're a St. Francis statue
alone in the east
patio: Eyes closed, warming in
what little sun,
you hear mourning doves,
spring in the leaves
scuttling across brick.

The chemo should kill
what surgery missed,
you hear doctors say.
Wasps on the west
porch deny you
sunsets. You tell my mother
not to spray. You say
you can live without the view.

Light Housekeeping

My mother smooths the hair from your cheek,
checks the clock,
slips on surgical gloves.
Lifts your leg,
buttocks hanging like meat,
inserts the morphine.
You do not twitch.
She sits beside you,
strips off the gloves,
pulls back your nightgown,
rubs you, her mother,
on the shoulder.
Your left hip,
skin stretched across bone,
stabs into the bed
and because my mother is sure
it pains you,
she cushions it with a pillow.
Each of your breaths
like a long-distance runner's
slides your teeth forward.
My mother takes them out,
sponges your mouth with water.
Your lips are blinds
flapping in an indifferent breeze.
My mother crosses to midmorning light,
widens the curtain.
Sparrows skirmish over millet.
I watch you, my grandmother,
your arm over your eyes like a child,
protecting what those close to death dream.

SECTION FOUR

Himmel

I — 1965

I lean on the branch,
rough like my mother's
heel I rub

reading my mystery.
Mockingbird, wings
shuffling air

like Liberty cards,
chases away a mourning dove.
My twin bangs open

the library door,
calls me down.
It's 11:15 on the Tucson Federal

S&L Building, where a father of four
jumped last week. Swim practice
in 15 minutes. We straggle down

a palm tree corridor,
reach a clearing of swings,
kick off our thongs.

Twist tight and twirl.
His washed-out picture
in the morning paper

like our father's:
crewcut, dark-rimmed glasses,
a man smiling

a father's bloodless lips.
We pump and pump,
legs sticking into sky,

white clouds coming down.
I see his children
walk their collie.

My sister leaps from the swing,
catches two thorns in her heel.
We pick at them like surgeons,

cool our soles in the changing
room shower. She cannonballs,
I sit on the edge.

A giant blue
sucks her in, spits her out.
She grins. I hang

onto the side,
my legs shimmer,
disappear

and reappear. She jumps
again. The father settled
claims. Small shock waves

slip over. Through the chain-
link I see
his children

play alone,
pretending to be men.

II — 1975

Furtively, he squeezes
breasts under my Made in
France glitter

t-shirt. I've kicked off
my platforms, stuffed
my bra in my purse.

Below us
they perform "Midsummer
Night's Dream" in the nude,

bongs bobbing
in darkness
like Chinese lanterns.

My boyfriend, headed
for Princeton, the school's
highest scorer,

drops the condom
in grass. A groundskeeper's
flashlight

wanders over us
midclutch. My
boyfriend sighs: a balloon

collapsing in a small
whoosh.

III — 1985

Dead of winter,
my friends and I
take roll call:

who's divorced,
who's had an abortion,
who's in rehab.

My high
school boyfriend
is dying of AIDS.

Corporate interviews
in the morning.
Co-workers lob

softballs in the afternoon,
fuck strangers at night
in the Parks &

Rec restroom. The next time
it'll be a vice cop.
Someday, someone will restore

the pool. Shower heads — shriveled
sunflowers — dangle at each
changing room exit. A body,

not my sister's, lies in weeds
a week before it is found.

IV — 1995

Barefoot and alone,
everything I need
in my VW,

I stand in dichondra
trying to remember
if the straight-beaked bird

was thrasher or mocking.
A young girl lifts a soccer ball
high and I

run to return — her mother calls out —
it hits a tree,
bounces back. The girl

smiles, thanks me anyway.
I smile back, say
no problem. I see my twin

in the curve of her face.
In the distance
under olive trees, a sculpture

for *los desaparecidos* rusts.
Five or six teens
huddle in a circle nearby,

tattoo each other's
ankles. Late afternoon,
warm adobe

walls the park. The girl
and her mother,
smoke twirling

from barbecue,
sit down to supper.
A sign says,

Pool to reopen soon.
I move on.

Also by Rebecca Dyer

"Sanctuary: Love Poems"

Available on Amazon.com

Praise for "Sanctuary: Love Poems" …

In "Sanctuary: Love Poems," Rebecca Dyer finds her inspiration primarily from friends, family, and the worlds in which she lives. The poems in this volume are renderings of lovely human figures interchanging their influences with the natural world, as well as with those of the highly focused witness herself. This poet is unafraid of her vulnerability as she has discovered its ultimate worth in how "A cloud breaks,/splinter of sunlight/strikes your heart like flint." Many of these poems reveal a preservation of beauty, and others, the destruction of what couldn't be maintained, and still more, the recurrent discovery of the need for a necessary yielding for the other's sake, a benefit to all. If you love the sensuous and the reflective, you'll love reading these poems.

— ***Poet Jeannine Savard, author of "Accounted For"***

I remember the sculptor John Waddell lamenting "Do Not Touch" signs, declaring that art, certainly his art, was meant to be touched. Just as pictorial art demands reaction from the eye, so do Rebecca Dyer's poems; but they also demand to be touched. Once touched, they invite the other senses, as well as the Other senses.

— ***Poet Richard Fenton Sederstrom, author of "Disordinary Light"***

Inner and outer experiences flow together in Rebecca Dyer's "Sanctuary," where she achieves a fine balance between the realm of feeling and that of sight and touch. She has created love poems which are firmly located in time and place, in a way that carries them beyond the obvious.

— ***Poet David Chorlton, author of "The Taste of Fog"***

Praise for
"What We've Come Here For" ...

There is an intricacy in "What We've Come Here For" that makes the journey through each poem a pleasure. People blend into their physical settings as we encounter them, but are always highlighted by a deft sense of observation.
— *Poet David Chorlton, author of "The Taste of Fog"*

Rebecca's poems enlarge me and comfort me.
— *Poet Frances New, author of "Gift from Maurice"*

Rebecca Dyer is a poet, journalist and teacher living in Arizona with her husband, Rick. Rebecca and her husband are co-editors of *The Blue Guitar* literary and arts magazine, *The Blue Guitar Jr.* literary and arts magazine for children and teens and *Unstrung* poetry magazine, all non-profit projects of the non-profit Arizona Consortium for the Arts. Contact the poet at RebeccaDyerPoetry@gmail.com.

www.ingramcontent.com/pod-product-compliance
Lightning Source LLC
Chambersburg PA
CBHW022343040426
42449CB00006B/700